Persuasion
& Reverse
Psychology

A powerful Vehicle to Succeed in your Life

Johanna Louise Lee

Table of Contents

Introduction

We have seen that the ability to persuade is one of the most crucial ingredients in our dealings with people if we want to influence others and do not want to be relegated to camp follower's role for the rest of our lives. The greater we can persuade others, the better we will be in whatever field we are pursuing, be it social, business, or recreational.

At first glance, some of the tactics we have looked at may seem manipulative, but we soon see that persuasive people are sensitive to others' needs and feelings when examined in greater depth. And to remain in roles where they continue to have the most significant influence, they need to generate high levels of loyalty and respect. Doing this requires sensitivity, integrity, and excellent communication skills.

It is not sufficient to simply persuade people to follow you once or twice. To gain influence, we need to establish ourselves as persuasive on an ongoing basis. This requires trust, credibility, and a high degree of empathy for the needs of others.

We have seen the result of fear generated persuasive techniques used by dictators and despots the world over. In the long term, these tactics always crumble and leave behind deep bitterness and hate.

Chapter 1:

How to daily excel in persuasion

Fake "sales"

Y ou know how you'll go to a store and they'll have labels with all the supposedly marked down prices? They show you several higher prices that have been crossed out, leaving the new price so you can compare it to the old ones.

In comparison, the new price seems like a bargain, but little does the customer know that the "old" prices never existed. They just print fake, higher prices that they cross out to trick you into feeling like you're scoring a deal, when really, you're just being played.

Car salesmen

It's common knowledge that car prices are jacked up to high heavens, and still, car salesmen will swear up and down that they're making you a massive discount by shaving a couple hundred off the sticker price. It's the price they got it for from the manufacturer, they swear!

In reality, not only is that not a real discount, they're still making a good chunk of cash off you. But do customers stop to think about that? No, not really.

They allow themselves to be swayed by how generous the salesperson is being and jump on the "deal". Meanwhile, the salesman is cackling in the background and twirling his dirty mustache while counting their money.

Ask for something outrageous

You know that method every teenager has used at least at some point, when they have bad news? Give the parents some really horrible piece of news and then just go "I'm kidding", so by the time you tell them the real thing, they'll just be relieved? Well, if you've ever done that, congratulations, you were employing a psychological persuasion technique and you didn't even know it!

The logic behind it is kind of the same as with the anchor; give someone something worse to compare to and then ask what you were really going to ask, so that in comparison, it seems minor, doable, reasonable, *etc.*

So, let's say you need to ask your friend for a ride somewhere. Start by asking if you can borrow their car to take on vacation next week because you just totaled yours. Understandably, they'll say no. But wait, can they at least drive you to your doctor's appointment tomorrow? They'll say yes, and I'll tell you why:

a) In comparison to that other request, this one seems super reasonable

b) They're relieved you moved on from the other request so quickly and that they can do something else to help you, instead

c) They feel bad about refusing you again in 20 seconds, so they'll say yes to ease their guilty conscience

Street beggars

"Hey man, can I have $100?" You probably won't give it to them, unless you're maybe having a really good day. But if then they turn around and say "Then can I have that sandwich?", you're much more likely to then give them your half-eaten sandwich. Hell, you'll even throw in $5, because you do feel bad for them.

Sometimes, asking for something ridiculous is a good way to get someone's attention, or shock them enough to throw them off balance for a second. Then, while they're still in that uncertain, "what just happened" state, you ask for something else, something much smaller, and they might just hand it right over. I ain't saying it's right, but hey, it works.

Children

If you have children – or just ever shopped with one – you know that they're constantly pulling at your clothes or hands, asking for stuff, trying to steer you towards the candy isle, having meltdowns, asking if they can have this and that toy, *etc.* It's insanity and parents are overwhelmed.

A kid might ask for something like a cake, or a $300 toy, eliciting the absolute refusal of the parent. But then they ask if they can at least have Smaller Candy Bar or Comparatively Much Cheaper Toy and the parent relents without much of a fight. Smart move, kid.

Asking for directions

When someone stops you in the street to ask for directions on how to get someplace, you don't think twice before explaining where they need to go. However, chances are that after that they'll either ask you if you want to accompany them or perhaps, you'll even volunteer to take them. You didn't realize it at the time, but you got persuaded.

Asking for money

Now, this one is tricky, but it can be pulled off, so pay attention. Let's say you need to borrow some money. But first, you need to scope out the situation and see who has it and who's willing to lend it to you. So, you go and ask a friend for a small sum of money. They have it and they give it to you. But see, you actually need more. Would they be so kind as to lend it to you?

In theory, they could say no, but they won't. They've already said yes and agreed to help you out, so refusing you now would mean leaving you in a lurch and no one wants to do that to their friend.

Plus, chances are they're too embarrassed to tell you they've changed their mind and are backing out.

Petitions

You know when someone comes around the office or something and they have a petition they need people to sign? If enough people sign it, then everyone else will as well, even if they don't believe in the cause.

Everyone already did, and they're terrified of being the odd one out and being the only one who didn't.

Donations

The same rules apply: a box goes around and everyone puts some money in. Yes, (almost) everyone, because they've seen everyone else do it, so they feel the social pressure, obligation or shame to do it as well. After all, if everyone can spare a dollar, they should be able to, as well, right?

Pitching in for gifts

It's someone's birthday at the office or in your group of friends and there's a card going around for people to sign and a collection for a gift. Everyone needs to pitch in. And everyone does, because they're too embarrassed not to. They look at the card and see so many names signed and that bag of money is full and really, no one needs their contribution, realistically, but they're going to give it anyway, because they feel like they have to.

Asking for donations

Sometimes, people who want your money will give you something in exchange for it, except they'll offer it to you beforehand, under the guise of a gift. Only after you've accepted whatever t-shirt or free pens and notepads, they gave you will they conveniently mention that they support a cause that is in need of donations.

What are you going to do, refuse now? No, you won't, because you'll be too embarrassed. You feel like you owe them because they gave you a "gift" (that you're paying for) and it's not like you'll give it back now because you're so stingy that you don't want to make a donation.

So instead, you'll go into your pocket and take out a $5 bill and stick it in the donation bin. Donation seeker: 1, You: 0. But hey, they've taught you a super valuable lesson, so you're the one who's actually the one who wins.

Fashion

This happens with a lot of celebrities, but over the last few years, it's been the case with Kate Middleton. Once she's photographed wearing something, that garment will be sold out within days or even hours. This happens for two reasons:

a) People feel like if they have something she has, then they're closer to being just like her; it's a way for them to connect and relate to her. It can be a thrill to own something just like the one the person you admire has.

b) People feel like the garment (or object, or anything else, really) has her stamp of approval, and if she wears it, then it must be outstanding. Because people see her as aspirational and an authority in dressing well, looking classy, being royal, *etc.* her picking out something to wear is essentially the same as her recommending it to everyone. So they all go out and buy what she does.

Marketing

How many ads have you seen that state those magic words "As seen on TV", or "As seen on X actress", or some website? At first glance, it doesn't seem relevant; why do I care that this product was featured in some other place? Oh, but it is relevant. You see, that's the stamp of approval we were talking about earlier. That says "Look, this authoritative source thinks this product is great, so buy it!". That convinces a lot more people than you think.

This is also another instance of that herd mentality I mentioned. Everyone else is using this, so I need to use it too, or at least try it to see what all the fuss is about.

So, let's assume you're trying to persuade someone to invest in your start-up idea. Telling them that X, Y, and Z have already invested or expressed their approval will make this other person more likely to also invest, because who are they to crap all over these other people's opinion? If they said it's good, then it must be true!

Sad movies

People love to cry. It's true, we like to feel sad and have a good cry sometimes, so we torture ourselves with terribly sad movies. This need is so pervasive, that filmmakers have caught on, and if they feel like getting an Oscar, all they have to do is include some unbearably sad event, preferably inspired by real life. It seems silly, but it's essentially a recipe for success.

I'm sure you've heard of women going to see a movie just to cry, probably a romantic one where the lovers are separated and one of them invariably dies at the end, leaving the other one behind, heartbroken. Why do you think Titanic is so popular? Is it because it's a good movie? No, not really. It's because it exploits a real tragedy and then adds another fictional one on top of that. Can you hear the money rolling in? Ka-ching!

Organized religion

Spirituality, personal beliefs, and everyone's private relationship with divinity are all well and good. Everyone believes in something and that something provides comfort and support in moments of great trial throughout our lives. Organized religion, however, is a more insidious safety net, as it relies on exactly the concept I just talked about.

Think about it; wouldn't it be nice to have someone else tell you what to do? To have everything already figured out and thought through – who you are, what you should do, what your personal journey is and how to stay on the right path, what the right path even is, *etc.* It's a seductive thing, because it allows you to shut off, somewhat, and follow the beat of someone else's drum.

This is why it's so important for the preachers to have incredible persuasive skills; their job is to convince all these people that are coming into their church every day for guidance and comfort.

They have to be convincing; they have to be authoritative and they have to look and sound like the real deal, otherwise the whole thing falls apart and people lose their way.

Vacation packages

You might be looking at this and thinking "Wait, how is this mind control? It's just a good deal". Ok, but think about it – you have this travel company offering you these "deals" out of the goodness of their hearts. You pay in exchange for having them think about and organize everything and you don't have to lift a finger.

Sure, it sounds great. But you didn't get anything you actually wanted, did you? They chose your location for you, the hotel you're staying in, the restaurants or the food you eat, the sights you'll be seeing, your transportation, *etc.* You come back and you think "Wow, that was a great vacation", but was it? Did you want this vacation or were you manipulated into thinking you did?

These companies don't pick these packages at random, they have quotas and they'll push certain things on clients instead of others if they need to sell more rooms in a certain hotel, for example. Or they don't have enough people going to a certain resort, so they send you over. You're not getting your dream vacation; you're getting their cast-off discount vacation.

Advertising

Subliminal messages and putting ideas into your head via words of agreement and questions is an old stand-by of advertising. Think of taglines like "Aren't you tired of subpar products?", or "Looking for a new car?", "Don't you deserve something beautiful?", "Don't you think it's time for a new washing machine?".

What they all have in common is that they're introducing ideas to you, that you haven't actually thought of on your own, and prompting you to agree. Ideally, your response would be "Yes, I was looking for X, Y, Z" or whatever they're trying to get you to buy.

It's a very effective advertising technique because it's very suggestive and it's easy for the consumer to think they came up with the idea that they need whatever product they saw in the ad.

Bonus mind control points if the ad also justifies this new purchase by saying you deserve it. You know people will embrace that thought wholeheartedly.

Suggesting something to your spouse

Let's say you want to buy a new car. You know your partner is not likely to go for it, but you have a seemingly absent-minded discussion with someone on the phone that he can overhear.

This person is buying a new car and it has so many advantages! It was so affordable, too! They really needed a new car; it was as old as yours.

This plants a seed into their head. Next, you'll maybe turn up the volume when a car ad comes up on TV, so they can listen to it clearly. Maybe comment about what a good deal it is, if someone was in the market for a car.

You can procure some brochures and leave them somewhere they'll be found, detailing some offer for the car you want. Soon, your significant other will come up with a brilliant idea – how about you buy a car? Make sure to praise them for thinking of it.

Business Negotiation

Negotiation for business agreements may use some of the same concepts of persuasion as personal negotiations, but the rules are entirely different. As we said earlier if you value the relationship with the person, you're negotiating with you must be prepared to lose. Pushing for the best possible outcome for your side isn't worth the loss of a friendship or the splitting of a family.

In business though, the gloves come off. That doesn't necessarily mean that you pursue a 'scorched earth' policy in a business negotiation. The time and expense in trying to bring that negotiation to a close probably won't be worth the effort in the end.

Making sure both sides come away from the bargaining table with a win is not just better from an ethical standpoint; it's simply more efficient because you can complete the deal so much more quickly.

To get the best deal, learning how to use the 6 Principles effectively will give you the best advantage during negotiations. But before negotiations start, you need to do your homework to get the most from your persuasive efforts.

Ways to Positively Influence Others in Your Workplace

It doesn't matter how hard you work or how brilliant you are, you cannot succeed in anything without cooperation from other people. We are not only individuals; we are all connected to one another in some way.

The world is actually shrinking as, at the touch of a button, the click of a mouse, we can keep up with and keep in contact with even the most remote parts of our globe, and we can learn from other cultures as easily as we learn from our own.

No matter which part of the world we come from, we are not so different. We all have the same needs, as does any stranger that we meet. The same thing can also be said about the people that we work with.

It doesn't matter where you work, and it doesn't matter what you do for a living. We all have one thing in common – a large part of our waking hours are spent in our workplaces, some of us in jobs that we like and some in jobs that we hate.

If you are the latter, if you are working at a place or doing a job that you simply don't like, you can make your life much more bearable by persuading people to be on your side. You might even find that you quite enjoy going to work after all.

Here are 10 ways that you can positively influence other people in your workplace and make life so much easier to bear:

Be Grateful

Or at least get into the habit of being grateful. Before you leave home every morning, look around at what you have and say the words "thank you." Be thankful that you have a home, maybe a car, food on the table and a family to share it with. Once you learn to appreciate what you have, your purpose will become much clearer – to bring home the money to pay for it all, the money that the job you hate pays you every week or month. As the day goes on and you face challenges that seem insurmountable, reflect on your gratefulness. It will make you happier, and it will make it easier for you to carry on.

Be Happy

Happiness truly is contagious, and there are, in all truthfulness, more than a billion reason to be happy. We weren't put on the earth to be miserable, so find a reason to be happy. Rejoice in the sky, the sun, the rain that gives life. Talk to your colleagues, the people who help you through each day at work; smile at those who don't help you. If you are alive and healthy, then you are doing okay. If you are happy others will be happy too.

Keep on Smiling

Even if you don't feel like it. There is an old expression, "fake it until you make it" and it has never been truer, especially when things go wrong. No matter what is happening, no matter how bad you feel - smile, and you will feel better. If the boss is on your back, your co-workers are not pulling their weight, your computer crashed and wiped out everything you did, just smile. There is actually a scientific reason for it: smiling helps to release endorphins in the blood, and these are not called happy hormones for nothing. Smiling also eases tension, not just in you but in those around you as well. People will notice, they will begin smiling, and the tension will ease. You and you alone will have persuaded everyone that everything is ok, with just a smile. A powerful way to smile is to look up at the ceiling while opening your arms and your chest. This simple move will increase your testosterone level and will boost your mood.

Always Say Your Pleases and Thank Yous

Good manners get you a long way and help to build up better relationships. This isn't just about the workplace, this works anywhere you go, to a restaurant, the movies, the grocery store. Be polite and show manners and people will do what they can to help you. In the workplace, your colleagues will more be likely to help you out if you are polite and treat them with the respect and courtesy you expect from them. Good manners show that you care so make it a habit of treating others as you want to be treated.

Steer Clear of the Gossip

At any given moment of the day, something will be happening in your workplace that gives people a reason to talk, to gossip about someone else behind their back. It is human nature to talk about things that happen, but the nature of gossip is that it often becomes distorted, purely for entertainment value. Gossip is demoralizing to the subject, and it can also be classed as bullying if it turns malicious. If you happen to be in a place where people are gossiping, and they try to draw you in, just smile at them and then walk away. Show them you will not become involved and avoid the negativity. Not only does it keep you stabilized, but it will also stop you from, wrongly, judging the victim and will also gain you respect from others.

Be Nice to the "Village Idiot."

It doesn't matter where you work, there will always be the "village idiot." This is perhaps a very cruel term because the victim of that term is, more often than not, merely eccentric, different from others, not so articulate. It doesn't make them an actual idiot. Whenever you have cause to speak to them, be nice to them, listen to what they have to say, and you might just be surprised at how un-idiot like they actually are. Too often, we label people unfairly and, by taking the tie to include them, to listen to them, you are developing a large amount of good will. You don't know when you may need to call on people for help, so make sure you keep them on your side.

Be Diplomatic

Everywhere you go, there will be people who say or do things that cause irritation. The real key is to stay objective and to stay calm. Losing your temper, or choosing to be angry as your very first reaction will do nothing more than providing the fire with a much-needed fuel source to keep on irritating you. Allow it to happen, and your colleagues will lose all respect for you. It doesn't matter how hard it is not to respond, when people say things that are hurtful or simply irritating, do not respond. Remain in control, remain calm, and you will be left alone. If you can muster one, smile at them and then continue with what you were doing. And if you do have to say something, keep your voice soft and be kind to them. It is your anger that they want, and if you don't give it, they have nothing. You, on the other hand, will gain the respect of your colleagues. Always be non-reactive.

Do Your Very Best All of the Time

Your bosses and any colleagues who are influential will respect you more if you always do the very best that you can. Even if you are at odds with people, doing your best, putting in your effort, will result in milestones being reached and deadline met. People may not like you for one reason or another, but they can still respect you for being someone they can depend on, someone who remains focused. You will also have a better sense of self-worth and purpose. It may result in a raise or promotion, or it could just mean that you are in a better position to influence others in the future.

Always Be Honest

Honesty is always the very best policy, and when you add diplomacy into the mix, you have the makings of a great communicator, a true leader. When you are trying to talk to others about your ideas, keep to the facts; don't throw in a lot of technical jargon and don't try to be too smart – it will backfire on you. Never exaggerate your claim, and never embellish them as people can see through that and your chances of persuading them round to your way of thinking will be gone. It isn't always the contents of the message that work; it is the way the message is conveyed.

Respect Other Cultures

The world is multicultural and, no matter where you live and work, you will come across people of different ethnicities and different cultures. Get to know them, get to know their traditions, beliefs, food choices and develop respect for them. Each different ultra has something that we can all learn from, and it is our moral duty to show them respect. Walk away from racist conversations; if you stay, if you join in, you are no better than they are.

Having that kind of name does not help you to be able to influence others, and everyone will lose a little of their respect for you. No matter where you go, no matter which nationalities you come across there will be good people and bad. Focus your energies on the good in all of us, and you will find that people are more prepared to cooperate with you, to follow where you want to lead them.

These may not seem like ways to persuade people but think about everything I have said carefully. By being nice to others, showing respect and remaining calm and dependable, you are turning yourself into someone that others will trust in, that they will want to follow. This is an essential part of powerful leadership

Chapter 2:

Persuasion in Relationships and Sex

Persuasion in close personal relationships can be a tricky business. Nobody likes to be manipulated or be in a relationship where they are not treated as an equal. It's important to focus on respect for the other person you are trying to persuade if you want them to stay in your life.

Using persuasion in these areas require that you focus on benefiting the other person while still getting what you want.

Persuasion in Dating

Trying to make sure you do what you can during that first meeting so that he or she is more likely to see you again is not a bad thing. Don't use persuasion to hide your 'true self' from the other person either, because that will show through eventually, and you might both end up miserable. Call these tips a way to put yourself in the best light.

Applying the 6 Principles

The 6 Principles of Persuasion can offer clues to dating as well. After all, a lot of what you're doing when trying to get someone interested in you is closely related to sales. How can some of these principles be used (in a non-creepy way) to persuade someone to spend time with you?

Scarcity

We're all familiar with the term 'playing hard to get.' That is the Principle of Scarcity in a nutshell. When someone sees that something is scarce or only available for a limited time, they are more likely to want it. To make yourself a scarce commodity, you might not agree to the first time someone is free or make your time available to meet for coffee limited because of your schedule. Some experts recommend being seen in the company of someone who could be competition to denote scarcity. You also might limit your time when you first meet, noting that you "were just on your way out." This time limit makes a good time to get someone's phone number, or even offer to have them go with you to another place to carry on the conversation. This time limit can make a decision in your favor more likely.

Social Proof

Make yourself known at your favorite restaurants, bars, and coffee houses. Get to know people by name and introduce yourself to them. When people get to the point of recognizing you on sight, like a returning friend, you have an asset that you can use to your advantage.

We all tend to like people that other people do. Restaurants and bars are no exception. When meeting someone new, suggest meeting at one of these favorite places. Even introduce them to the staff, and make them 'part of the club,' too. When the staff seems to know and like you, it asks as social proof to your prospective mate and allows them to feel more comfortable. If everybody seems to be treating you special, he or she will be more inclined to do so as well.

Reciprocation

Giving someone, something makes you more likely to get something in return, and this can work in getting that first date. If you have a business card or personal card with your info on it, offer it to that special someone before you go. Most people will take it from you just out of reaction. Then wait for theirs. The wait will prompt them to do something. Offer your phone, or have them shoot you a text right then, to make sure you get it. They may give you the number of their insurance agent, or if they are interested, you'll help them to decide to provide you with their contact info.

Commitment and Consistency

If you do get that number, follow up with another attempt at a 'yes.' Ask for a relaxed meeting for coffee, or an event. Just a chance to talk longer isn't hard to commit to, and if you have already gotten the agreement started, the Principle of Commitment and Consistency tells us they are more likely to agree again.

Persuasion for Commitment

The most significant commitment most of us will make in our lives is to commit spending the rest of that life loving and caring for another individual. That's a big decision, and once we've made it, we hope that our partner will make it, too.

Can we persuade someone to make that kind of commitment? And more importantly, once we have persuaded them to commit, can we use persuasion techniques to help them stay committed? The commitment should be a product of an internal desire and free will, so overtly persuading someone to become or remain committed to you can be manipulative. Forcing someone is abuse. But there are ways that you can commit to treating another person that will make them more likely to *self-persuade* themselves into committing to you and treating you in a loving and caring way as well. That's a great way to build a long-lasting relationship.

Subtle Cues of Caring

Keeping someone committed to you for the long-term means telling them you love and care for them. Telling them verbally is great, but you can't do that constantly. But you can adopt behaviors that communicate regularly in a non-verbal way just how you feel. Once you start making these parts of your regular habits, you find that your partner will begin to respond in a more loving and caring way as well.

The first thing we all can do is to pay a little more attention to our physical appearance. When you were trying to get that special someone to notice you, or when you went on that first 'real' date, didn't you take a little extra time to make sure you looked great? Once we've been with someone a while, that attention may start to wane. This can even lead to a loss of intimacy. While you can't look great 24 hours a day, seven days a week, you can make the extra effort regularly to show you still care enough to be attractive.

Regular acts of attentiveness or love work to show your love as well. Small things that you did when you were dating — holding the door, kissing, touching and caressing — all show you *still* care. Being in a relationship with someone gives you hundreds of opportunities regularly to show someone how you feel about them. I know some people who pet the dog more than they touch their partner. That is a way to make a relationship go the **wrong** way. If you're unsure what to do, think about the things that make you feel loved. Use of the right non-verbal cues regularly can help continue to convey your desire to stay in a relationship. Not doing them can make your relationship sour.

In addition to body language and environmental factors, directly applying some of the 6 Principles can further your relationship also. Let's take a look at a few.

Liking

Okay, maybe this seems obvious, but look at your daily actions with your partner. Are you still trying to get them to like you, or do you merely think you have that part 'locked in'? Now really pay attention to your partner. Do they **act** as if they like you? I'm not talking about speaking civilly here. People at the grocery store do that. Can you **tell** that they like you? Do they want to spend time with you?

If not, it's time to get to work on the Principle of Liking. Your partner isn't going to stay in a relationship with someone they don't like. Think back to when you first met and think of the way you acted to make him or her smile. What did you do to get **that look**? Try doing more of that, and see if it doesn't persuade them to give you that look again, and be more likely to commit to you for the long haul.

Commitment and Consistency

We're talking about starting or keeping a long-term commitment, so how do we use the Principle of Commitment and Consistency to achieve that? It's simpler than you may think.

We know that people like to act in a way that is consistent with how they see themselves. To improve their commitment, remind them of the good times you've **already** had together. Use mental pictures to talk about what you could be if you stay together in the future. Research says that using the word "imagine" will help kick-start your mate's imagination, helping them to see the beautiful future you're describing vividly. This will persuade them to act in a way that is consistent with getting to that future **with you.**

Consistency also means that people are more likely to keep things as they are. Your mate might respond in a positive way to an imagined future, but the research also says that they will react even more strongly to avoid loss. When you're out at one of your favorite places, mention how you would never want to lose moments like this. Stressing the avoidance of loss from time to time can reinforce the happiness of the commitment they've made.

Reciprocation

Making your feelings of commitment known first can get the desired response back in return. Especially in emotional subjects, people have a great fear of rejection. Making the first move in areas where you are looking for confirmation can help to alleviate that fear in your mate and let them know that they are not alone in the feelings. This may make you the vulnerable one, but it may be the only way to get the discussion going in the right direction if you want a long-term commitment. Based on the Principle of Reciprocation, the odds are in your favor that you'll receive a positive reaction in return.

Chapter 3:

The Psychological theories of

Influence and Persuasion

Conversion Theory

This theory majorly applies to groups where there is a majority and a minority. It becomes easy for a minority group to get members from the majority group simply because most of them are just moving with the masses, are not strong believers in its cause, or they just lack an alternative.

The minority have the courage to show how different they are by confidently opposing them.

The minority gets its power from:

- Resistance of the social pressure always brought about by the majority members.

- Being both unbiased and reasonable while presenting their ideas.

- Being sure about their ideas and the views they present, and

- Showing consistency in how they express their opinion.

Example

Large groups of workers in an organization are dissatisfied with newly implemented rules on how to discipline lawbreakers. They think the rules are crazy and they are threatening to go on strike. However, a small group is okay with the rules. Through the members of this small group, the management board peacefully engages key leaders of the majority group in a reasonable and persuasive conversation giving them a better perspective to look at the rules. The majority leader's change their mind and convince their members too.

How to Use It

If you are in the minority group, get more people who think along your line of thought and help them build their confidence, consistency, and straightforwardness then let them help you spread your voice of reason.

Defending

Be smart enough to notice when the minority is about to start up against you and use you as the majority leader. Expose their methods to your followers and let them be aware. At times, you will experience situations where the masses disagree with your opinion. Being a minority is hard; nonetheless, even in these situations, you can do something to convert the majority in your favor, use the conversion theory.

The conversion theory states you can make the majority budge from their stance because quite often, many people in the majority group are not strong believers in their stance. They may be going along with the idea because it seems easier to follow and adopt, or because there lacks a substantial alternative. It is also possible that they are disillusioned with the group's main purpose, leadership, or process and are in search of a better substitute.

To convert the majority in your favor, here is what you have to do.

Stay Consistent

First, stay consistent with your opinion and do not negate your stance at any cost.

Be Confident

Secondly, gain command over the topic so you can be confident in what you believe in.

Stay Unbiased

Thirdly, be unbiased and reasonable. Instead of strongly favoring your approach, hear the ideas of the majority and then use logical reasoning to prove them wrong.

Offer Resistance

Fourthly, keep resisting the social abuse and pressure the majority members inflict upon you.

To help you understand this theory better, here is an example:

An extremist group in your area believes there should be a law against fracking. The majority disagrees with them, but they maintain their stance. They hold peaceful demonstrations against your area's local government on a regular basis. They engage passersby in persuasive and reasonable conversations and get them to sign a petition that shows they have the vote of the majority in their favor.

When you belong to the minority and want to turn the majority in your favor, this strategy is helpful. To execute this strategy successfully, you need to have complete command over the viewpoint you advocate for and do not lose your confidence under any pressure situation.

Another effective theory that works its magic on mass persuasion is the social impact theory.

Social influence Theory

This theory proposes that the chances you will respond to any sort of social influence increase with three factors:

Strength

How strongly people influence you or how important these people are to you.

Immediacy

How closely related you are to that group.

Number

The number of people in the group.

If you are close to an influencing group, the group is important to you, and has many people; the group will easily influence you. The social impact theory/technique is especially useful when you want to convince someone of your opinion or belief, but you know the person will not budge unless you have some support.

For instance, if you want your son to quit smoking, you may first try convincing him yourself, and then collaborate with his father, friends, and other people he trusts to make him quit smoking.

To practice this theory, first try to persuade that person. As you do that, look for people your target trusts and to convince that person, collaborate with these people. Keep adding more supportive people to your group until the person eventually succumbs to the pressure exerted by the large group.

Attribution Theory

Human actions can be clarified by one of two attributions, situational or dispositional.

Situational

This has also been referred to as "external" attribution. According to this provenance, there are certain things outside of a person's control that impact their behavior. For example, claiming a person cannot be held responsible for the situation they are in because it was bad before they became embroiled in it, is an application of situational attribution.

Dispositional

This has also been referred to as "internal" attribution. The premise of this attribution is that human actions can be explained by a person's disposition, motive, traits, or abilities. For example, claiming because a person lacks certain knowledge or has a particular personality trait, such as greed or laziness, that is the reason for the current state of affairs, is an application of dispositional attribution.

Another person's behavior is most often explained or sought to be understood by dispositional attribution rather than situational. This is true because we often do not fully grasp the external or outside situations surrounding a person, so we gravitate to the complexities of the individual's internal situations. When you are trying to explain yourself or seek for others to understand you, most people will try to persuade others by using dispositional attribution to highlight their achievements and positive behaviors and situational attribution to explain their negative behaviors and inadequacies.

Conditioning Theory

Direct commands are not the actions of a strong persuader. Instead, the aim is to guide people to take their own actions. This is part of conditioning, which is a major part of persuasion. Linking a positive motivation or value to a logo of a company is an example of conditioning. Over time, the messages of joy, sexual desire, or personal connection are shown within the logo. It is an attempt to connect with the audience. Another example is in political campaigns. If a candidate makes direct face-to-face contact with potential voters, and that contact is positive, that voter is more likely to vote for that candidate. We are also conditioned to associate a certain smell or sound with an item. Think of your grandmother's house. If she was fond of baking apple pies or having rose-scented potpourri, later in life, when you smell one of those smells in an unconnected event, you will think of her. You link this with a positive emotion. This is established over time and many exposures to the message, however subtle or overt it may be.

Cognitive Dissonance Theory

Introduced in the '50s, this theory claims that humans want their thoughts, attitudes, and beliefs to be regular. Despite wanting this regularity, our cognitions can swing from alignment to disparity, or between. The disparity between your beliefs, thoughts, or attitudes is called "dissonance." This makes us uncomfortable and feeling as if we are missing something.

For example, when you are diabetic and understand that eating excessively sugary foods is bad for you but do it anyways, you suffer from cognitive dissonance. Our natural inclination is to bring this dissonance into synchronization within our mind. We can bring our mental cognitions into alignment. Leon Festinger, the founder of this theory, identified four methods for creating consistent mental processes. These four steps are:

Change

Our attitude, beliefs, or thoughts need to be changed.

Reduce

The importance of a thought or belief needs to be condensed.

Increase

The difference between the dissonance needs to be minimized, bringing the two sides closer to one another.

Re-evaluate

A negotiation of the reward versus cost of the cognition needs to be reconsidered.

This means the diabetic can change their habit of eating sugary foods, reduce the impact on their health, decide they are not really at risk while eating these foods, or decide the cost of being healthy is not worth giving up the reward of the sugar-laced treat.

Functional Theories

Functional theorists attempt to understand how different situations impact the dissonance of someone's attitude regarding different objects or situations.

A function that is impacted by communication can be influenced by persuasion to various degrees.

Once a person is persuaded another action would fulfill the function better, the persuasion was a success. Attitudes typically have four main functions:

Knowledge

Control and understand your life by setting rules and standards that will manage your sense of self.

Value-expressive

We exhibit a version of ourselves that we want to align with who we want to be or what we want to believe. This exhibition gives us pleasure because it is aligned with our concept of ourself.

Ego-defense

People attempt to protect their own egos from personally threatening thoughts or negative impulses. We create processes to keep ourselves from experiencing these negative scenarios.

Adjustment

Decrease costs and increase affirmative exterior rewards. We choose to move from punishment to rewards with our behavior.

Information Manipulation Theory

Here, you, the persuasive person, deliberately break one of the four maxims of conversation where the following expectations thrive:

Manner

You express information in a manner easy to understand through the use of non-verbal actions.

Relation

Only give information relevant to the conversation.

Quality

You only give truthful and accurate information.

Quantity

You give the listener full information that he or she expects form you.

Example

A husband is late for a dinner date with the wife. He parks his car and approaches the table looking a little bit shaken with a (fake) ticket in his hand saying he has just been pulled over for a traffic offence – speeding – while rushing to get there on time. Otherwise he could have made it on time.

How to Use It

To apply the information manipulative theory, omit some information but include an element of truth in what you say. Be smart with your excuses. Confuse the other person by going off the subject a bit.

Defending it

If you find yourself changing your mind, question whatever excuse. Ask for evidence and be keen on the body language. Pay attention to every detail.

Inoculation Theory

This theory is just like the idea of giving a vaccine to prevent an illness that could invade the body. It may never happen, but by introducing a small amount of the virus, your body creates a defense against the disease, so if it does attack, you are prepared to fight it. To apply this to life situations, consider political parties. They may introduce an easily debunked argument to create the ability for their followers to ignore or dismiss a larger, stronger, or more developed argument from another party. Think about those negative advertisements. One political party may refute the claims of another so that when that opposite party makes those claims, the followers disregard them immediately.

Social Judgment Theory

We attempt to understand persuasive communication by sorting it subconsciously and reacting to it according to our own feelings. The attitude we already have determines how we compare and evaluate new information. This is our anchor point, or initial attitude. From this point, we decide if the persuasion falls into a realm we could accept, cannot accept, or one for which we have little interest. The closer the persuasion falls to their anchor point, the more acceptable it feels to the person.

The Rule of Reciprocity

The rule of reciprocity is simple but effective; when we think that we were given a gift or a favor, we immediately think that we have the obligation to give back to the giver. This applies not just in sales but also in all aspects of life. A business meeting between strangers for example, usually starts with the giving of gifts. Usually, the one who needs something usually gives the gift.

Political and economy experts call this type of interaction the gift economy. It is common in business, politics and international diplomacy. Tycoons, politicians and world leaders often give each other gifts to show that they are entering a relationship with good will.

The rule of reciprocity is hardwired in our mentality partly from the experience of our ancestors in the past. When rival tribes meet, the interaction often ends up in conflict. Even the stronger tribe would prefer that these types of interactions end without conflict for the safety of their members.

Eventually, when rival tribes met they offered each other gifts to prevent conflict and violence. Tribes that exchanged their goods coexisted, even in overlapping territories. Since then, the idea of gift giving has become one of the foundations of new relationships.

The rule of reciprocity also works in sales. A salesperson can use it to persuade his connections to do certain behaviors that will help them generate new sales. First though, the salesperson first needs to plan how they will approach these people.

This rule can be broken down into three important factors:

The Target

The target refers to the person who had been the recipient of a gift from you in the past. Your target should have certain qualities that could be advantageous towards your goal, which is to make more sales. An example would be targeting someone with a high status in a community where your target market mostly is located. If you are selling car insurance for example, you can target someone who manages car shows as well as other car salespeople.

For the target of the rule of reciprocity to cooperate in the system, certain criteria needs to be met:

First, the target should not expect the gift from you. This criterion should be met for two reasons. First, if there is an expectation for the gift, the target may not feel obliged to give back. If the target does not have this feeling, they're not likely to return the gift-giving practice.

The second reason for this criterion is that unexpected gifts are more memorable. In January of 2017, newly elected US president Donald Trump first stepped into the Whitehouse and was welcomed by the incumbent president Barrack Obama. Together with them were their wives, Melania Trump and Michelle Obama. In the ceremonial meeting, Melania Trump brought a blue box wrapped in ribbon and she presented it as a gift to her predecessor.

The media went wild over the gift-giving, not because of the nature of the gift but because of Michelle's reaction to it. When she was given the gift, she did'nt know what to do with it because it was not expected. In press events like these, the parties are expected to shake hands, have a few personal greetings to each other and have their picture taken. By giving her the gift there in public, Melania Trump unknowingly disrupted the flow of the ceremonial meeting.

Michelle Obama understood the importance of the event and the photo that follows. She knows that the picture will be an important part of history. It will be viewed in schools and in museums in the future. Her reaction wasn't that she was dumbfounded by the gift, but because of the inconvenience that it would make while the photo was being taken. It threatens to ruin a historical photo. Luckily for Michelle Obama, her husband quickly took the gift and brought it inside before the photo opportunity.

The significance of the gift in this case is not the nature of its content or even its value. It is lies on the memorability of the event of the gift giving process. In the days that followed, the media talked about the event a lot. A year after it was given, Michelle Obama even talked about the event in a talk-show and explained her puzzled reaction towards the gift. All this attention made the event and the gift giving even more memorable.

Because it is such a memorable occasion, we can expect that the rule of reciprocity is working between these two relationships. The public has a clear memory of Melania giving Michelle a gift. In their minds and possibly the recipient's mind, there is a need for the gift giving process to be returned. It would not be surprising if, in a future event where the press is present, Michelle also gave Melania a gift to finally close the rule of reciprocity.

The second criterion that needs to be met is about the intention of the target. For him or her to be cooperative in the gift economy, he or she should put some value in the relationship. The target should also want the relationship to continue. If you give a gift to a stranger and never meet that person again, the gift would'nt be returned in kind, and there would be no continuation in the rule of reciprocity.

This rule works best for people that you are likely to transact with again in the future. Ideally, the target should also have his or her own reasons for keeping the relationship alive. In our car insurance sales scenario above, the salesperson is more likely to successfully use this rule with someone who also gains something from the relationship. The insurance car salesperson for instance, could use this rule to build relationships with car salespeople. By building a relationship with each other, both parties will be able to have access to each other's contact people.

The Gift

The gift refers to the thing or act of service given to the target. The nature and even the value of the gift are of little importance. The most important feature of the gift is its memorability. If the gift is remembered, it is more likely to trigger a sense of obligation on the receiver of the gift.

The sense of obligation created because of the creation of the gift is the currency created by the interaction. Think of it as a lender-borrower kind of relationship. When a gift is given, there is a sort of debt that needs to be repaid. The gift and gift giving even should create a sense of obligation in the giver. This sense of obligation will only be created if the gift is not returned or if the recipient does not give a gift back to the giver.

For the gift to be memorable, it should also be given in an unexpected time. Gifts given in events where gift giving is expected do not trigger the rule of reciprocity. When you give a gift in a wedding for example, the wedding couple will thank you for it, but they will not be obliged to return the favor. The same goes when more than one person gives a gift. When you move into a new neighborhood for example, the neighbors a likely to give you a welcoming gift. However, because multiple people gave gifts, only the most memorable ones are likely to be remembered. Because most of the gifts are forgotten, they are not likely to create a sense of obligation in the receiver.

Acts of service can also trigger the sense of obligation that is necessary for this rule to work. When you do something for another person, you could use it as a bargaining chip when interaction with that person again in the future. This type of gift however, is not as obvious, compared to a tangible gift, creating the possibility that the recipient of the act will not recognize it as a gift. Tangible gifts tend are easy to notice and their presence reminds the recipient of the sense of obligation that they may have to the giver. Most acts of service do not have a tangible result. Because of this, there is nothing to remind the recipient of the act of their sense of obligation to the giver.

To make sure that your act is remembered by the recipient, you should emphasize it to them that you are doing them a favor. You could say that because you are friends you will do this favor for them. The idea of favors creates the sense of obligation in the mind of the other person. The idea is that they should also help you if you are the one in need.

The Request

The last part of the rule is the request. This refers to the thing or action that you will ask from the other person. This is your reward for giving something to your connections. When it is you who is in need, they are more likely to answer your plight for help.

However, with the rule of reciprocity, it is not just the altruistic nature of people that will make them act on your request. It is the sense of obligation that they need to give back something for accepting a gift from you.

The value and the memorability of the gift becomes the basis of the degree of f difficulty of the request. The people you helped in their time of dire need have a bigger sense of obligation to keep to the law of reciprocity. It also helps of the gift was given in public or in the presence of other people. The presence of other people in the giving of the gift puts social pressure on the recipient to also give a similar gift in kind.

As a salesperson, you should make use of the sense of obligations that you create in other people by using them to create more sales. While you could ask them to buy from you, you will have a higher degree of success if you ask them request that will not require them to spend money. You could use the people indebted to you to help you find prospect buyers for example.

You could also ask them to introduce you to important people that you could do business with in the future. The possibilities are endless when it comes to the types of requests that you can ask using the rule of reciprocity. Just remember that the bigger the request, the lower your chances of success will be.

How to establish the rule of reciprocity

The rule of reciprocity is a mental process that that naturally occurs in people. Many people are not aware that it exists. The ones who do know that it exists are likely to resist its effect. People can resist it because there is no legal basis bounding them to it. Instead, it is only their strong sense of obligation that keeps them abiding to the rule.

To set up the rule on anyone you know and to increase its level of success, you must follow these guidelines:

Choose your target wisely

Not everyone has a habit of giving back. Some people will just take from you and never give back favors, even if you ask them to. To be successful in setting up this rule, only use it with people who have a history of being generous and who are fond of giving back.

It is also important to choose people who have the power to help you back. If the person chooses to work with does not have the money to buy from you or does not have the connections to refer people to you, you cannot expect him or her to return any of the favors you give.

Lastly, you want to target people who will also benefit from the relationship that you are trying to build. Some people will not return favors because they don't want to work with you in the first place. Look for people who can benefit from having you as a friend. This could include people from another sales industry that complement yours, for example.

Make your gift giving subtle but public

When giving gifts, it is important that you make the process subtle, without announcing to the world. You should not mention the gift at all after giving it. The idea is not make a big deal out of it. However, you need to make sure that many other people see you when giving the gift. They don't need to see what the gift is.

The mere fact that they know that a gift was given puts pressure on the receiver to give back another gift to you. For most people, their reputation as a person who returns favors depends on it.

Add a personal note with the gift

Master gift givers know that personal notes make the gift even more memorable. This is the reason why all gift wrappers come with a card. You're meant to make a personal handwritten note to go along with your gift.

To make an impact with your note, try to add humor to it. If you have an inside joke with the receiver of the gift, use that for added impact. Any message will be better than having no message at all.

Give gifts or acts of service when the other person is in need

The value of a gift or a favor significantly increases when it is given at a time of need. When person is a low point in his or her life, they are more likely to remember the people who helped. Most people look back to this point in their lives even when they are doing much better. In the process, they're also likely to remember the people who helped them out in their time of need. When you see someone, you could do business within a bad situation, take the time to extend a helping hand. They will return the favor once they have recovered.

Do not be afraid of asking for favors

Lastly, you should not be afraid to ask for favors. When you are in need or when you need more business, look back to your list of people that you have established the rule of reciprocity with. Do not be afraid of asking them for favors. They have every right to say no to you. However, the rule of reciprocity is likely to compel them to help you out if they have the power to do so.

Using the 5 Love Languages with the Rule of Reciprocity

The problem with the rule of reciprocity it that not all your good deeds towards other will be considered as a favor or a gift that needs to be repaid. Beginners in selling who try to use this rule tend to waste a lot of money and time doing kind deeds to people who do not appreciate their actions. One way to make sure that your target person likes the thing or service that you shared is by using the so-called Love Languages.

Love languages come from the book of bestselling author Gary Chapman. In his book, he says that people experience and understand love in five different ways. He called these five ways the Love Language.

To be able to make a person feel loved, you should understand and cater to his or her love language. If you offer a different love language to a person, he or she is less likely to appreciate it. Chapman suggests that the five love languages include:

Words of Affirmation

Words of affirmation refer to the positive words that we use when dealing with a person. In a romantic relationship, words of affirmation can be shown by saying phrases like "I love you" to the other person. Among friends, words of affirmation can be shown by saying things like "I miss you" or "I really appreciate that you are in my life".

Acts of service

Acts of service refers to tasks and actions that you do for the other person. If a person has this love language, he or she is more likely to appreciate the things that you do for him or her. If that person is tired of his chores for example, you can make him feel loved by helping out with the chores.

Receiving Gifts

Some people also appreciate acts of gift-giving most of all. Just like the fact that they like giving gifts, they're also are likely to enjoy receiving them. The gifts don't need to be expensive or important. People with this kind of love language are likely to enjoy even smaller gifts that stand out.

Quality Time

People with this love language tend to value the time other people spend with them. A person who feels like quality time is important want to spend time with other people, preferably those who are most important in their lives.

If you want to gain the favors of a person with this type of love language, you should invite them to simple get-together events. You could for example, invite an old friend for coffee, just to catch up.

Physical Touch

Physical touch refers to physical connections between people. A person with this type of love language is likely to appreciate simple physical interactions with other people like a handshake, a pat in the back of a hug.

Priming

Priming refers to when a certain stimulus influences your responses long after exposure to the stimuli. To explain this, let me give you an example.

If someone gives you a list of words containing pet, cat, and wolf, then, someone later asks you to think of a word that rhymes with log, your most likely answer will be dog. The word 'wolf' will remind you of a dog; the word 'cat' usually pairs with dog and since a dog is a pet and rhymes with log, you are likely to give 'dog' as your answer.

As you can see, that little list directed your mind to select the word dog. This is how priming works. It works on your subconscious and produces an effect that usually lasts a day or two, but sometimes, this effect can last longer.

You can use the knowledge of this technique to become very self-observant. If you really pay attention, you will realize that most of our decision making happens on a subconscious level. Have you ever wondered why it just felt right to wear that blue shirt today, only to realize that your friend had just recently told you she was feeling blue? Have you wondered why you decided that you wanted to eat spaghetti for dinner, only to realize that you glimpsed an Italian travel billboard on your way home from work? If you really pay attention, you will realize that a tremendous amount of your actions have actually been predetermined for you based on the way your subconscious mind reacts to certain signals.

The first step to mastering this technique is to write down 2-3 examples of the priming technique working on you. How can you do this if you are not aware of it happening? Simple - when you make a seemingly random decision such as what song you want to listen to, stop and think to yourself: *Is there something that I picked up on subconsciously that is influencing me to make this decision?* I think you will be surprised to find that the most incidental things can have profound effects upon your decision-making process!

Technique 1: Priming

2-3 examples of priming experiences in your daily life

Unconscious priming aims to affect your word choice by manipulating your subconscious mind. You opt for certain words long after you feed these words into your mind.

Priming not only makes you recall certain words, it also makes you think of different ideas, concepts, memories, and thoughts by bringing similar ideas and thoughts to your awareness.

In effect, this technique either brings new things to your awareness or re-introduces old thoughts that lie close to your subconscious mind's surface and makes them easily accessible. For instance, when you buy a new car, you start to notice other cars similar to yours.

Amplification hypothesis

The 'agree and amplify' strategy is very helpful when you want to make someone budge from his or her stance. If you are in an argument with someone who strongly believes in his or her viewpoint and does not want to accept yours, the best way to make the person acknowledge and accept your viewpoint is by practicing the 'agree and amplify' technique.

Using this technique, you do not argue against that person's belief; neither do you try convincing the person of the wrongness in his or her opinion/viewpoint. Instead, you simply agree with the person's belief and then amplify his or her viewpoint and argument by connecting it with the person's beliefs and values.

You use logical reasoning to make your target understand how illogical his or her opinion is and then ask the person if the opinion still seems sensible.

When you see your target backing down, you do not dive in for the kill. Instead, you give the person a little time to reprocess his or her viewpoint and then ask him/her questions like, "So what does this imply, or are there other ways or viewpoints we can consider?" Once the person seems open to new ideas, you bring in your viewpoint and make the person accept it by backing it with logical reasoning.

Examples of 'Agree and Amplify'

Here are a few real life examples of agree and amplify: For instance, if you are talking to someone who believes dogs are a menace, someone who is against dogs when you love dogs, then you could use agree and amplify to open the person to the idea of being nice to dogs.

You could say, "Oh, you think all kinds of dogs are a complete nuisance and a menace? Hmm, I think it makes sense. After all, dogs are like wolves. How about we create laws to muzzle all dogs or ban dog ownership, does that seem right to you?" When you see the person's expression softening, you could gradually bring in your viewpoint: dogs are lovable. To help you understand 'agree and amplify', here is another real life example:

Your ten-year-old son demands an Xbox for his eleventh birthday. You want your child to give up the idea of getting an Xbox for his birthday and instead get something more useful he can use to complete school assignments, say for instance, an iPad.

To convince him, you could say, "I understand an Xbox is really important to you, after all, it lets you play amazing games even though it does not help you complete school assignments and you have to constantly beg your elder sister to lend you her laptop. That is all right, after all, an Xbox is not as great as an iPad that allows you to do work and play games too."

As you can see, this technique is a good way to convince people. Here is why this strategy is extremely powerful. This approach helps you use logic (proving the other person logically wrong) to convince people not to do something how they want to. Moreover, this technique helps you remind people of their values and beliefs, think reasonably, and opt for a measured approach.

When you realize a person's values and beliefs are not universal and do not produce the desired work in all types of situations, you become more open to perceiving things differently. In addition, as you realize it is possible to be wrong, your entrenched position becomes untenable, and you have to move forward to stay congruent with your new approach.

This strategy helps you broaden people's horizons and help them see things from different perspectives while making them agree with you. Here is how you can use this strategy.

Relative Anchoring

Another effective hypnotic persuasion technique is 'relative anchoring'. Relative anchoring means that to reach a conclusion, we often anchor our mind to a relative piece of information and iteratively adjust ourselves away from that information until we reach a conclusion/decision that seems logical and reasonable.

To explain this concept, let me give you an example.

Recall the last two digits of your mobile number. Do you have the digits in your mind? Now, simply think of the percentage of African countries in the UN (United Nations.) Is that percentage less or more than the last two digits of your phone number, how much less or more?

The way that you can practice this technique is to use it as a strategy in negotiation. To use relative anchoring correctly, always start a negotiation in a good way from your main stance. For instance, if you are selling your house, give a bigger quote than the actual market rate so a potential buyer makes an offer relative to your quote. However, if the buyer makes the first bid and it is close to the real price, do not settle for it.

If you are the buyer and the seller make a bid, do not assume it is close to the final price. Instead, make a very small bid so you bring the buyer's quote down. This way, you will use this technique in your favor. Practice using this technique and write down your experiences to solidify this concept in your mind.

Technique 7: Relative Anchoring

Results and Reflections

Now that you know the various effective persuasion techniques, let us now look at strategies you can use to influence people.

Chapter 4:

Your Attitude Change Approach

Ways to Change People's Perceptions—After All, Perception Is Reality

James is an exceptional deals director for a Fortune 500 organization. He considers himself to be active, inviting, quick moving—a genuine article producer. A portion of the general population he works with, however—and in addition, some of his customers—consider him to be a quick-talking backslapper and somewhat of an imposter. Which perception is accurate? Also, why does it make a difference?

The "perception is reality" proverb is regularly connected to the path each of us sees as our own condition. In the event that we see the glass as half full, we will work with that reality, and the glass will dependably be at any rate half full. Be that as it may, imagine a scenario in which we turn that saying back to front. Imagine a scenario in which the reality we're encountering is connected to some extent to how others see us.

How about we return to James for a minute. He considers himself to be an arrangement creator, however, of late, the arrangements have been becoming scarce. He's experiencing difficulty getting arrangements, never mind inspiring customers to return his telephone calls. What's more, the general population of his group is working without him, letting him alone for imperative discussions and meetings. James is in genuine need of a perception redress. So how would we make the "me" we need others to see? How would we change perceptions? There are various moves we could make, however, regardless of our normal conduct.

Request input

Ask others how they see you. It takes bravery, and you may get some input that is difficult to hear, yet it's an imperative stride in renewing your perception. Stay away from the temptation to discard what a person is stating, regardless of the possibility that it doesn't fit your viewpoint. Rather, plunge into the feedback. The more you comprehend about the other individual's perception, the better you can monitor, or even alter, it. Burrow further to comprehend their reasoning with the accompanying inquiries: - What is the effect of my conduct on you (or others)?

- What exhortation would you have for me to work/interact another way?

- Help me comprehend why you feel thusly.

- Roll out behavioral improvements quickly.

Once you have some essential data, step toward behavioral change. In case you're the sort who generally commands the discussion in meetings or gatherings, take a stab at keeping completely peaceful and taking notes for a change.

If you normally hang back and let others take the spotlight, record some key indicators that are pertinent to the theme being talked about and speak up. Perceptions won't change overnight, yet you will start to notice that others are responding in an unexpected way.

Up your visibility

If you need high visibility, you need to do what it takes to appear distinctly unmistakable. Begin by volunteering for high effect ventures.

Seek out that difficult assignment no one wants to handle, or something that has been mulling despite knowing it's critical to your supervisor or the organization overall. In the event that you see the organization putting a great deal of time and effort into another thought or effort, get included.

Search out open doors

Identify openings with different offices that will expand your visibility. For example, a venture or team that will allow you to see and be seen by individuals you wouldn't meet generally. Offer to make introductions or address groups at events, both inside and outside the organization.

Advance yourself

You may be the best representative on the planet, however, in the event that your commitments go unnoticed, it won't make any difference. You require individuals who will talk emphatically about you and your achievements. This can occur on many fronts; however, it starts when you speak up for yourself. This does not mean uncontrolled gloating about all that you do. It means sharing wins transparently and giving credit to colleagues and team members when it's due. Recount examples of overcoming adversity and praise achievements.

Search out promoters

Identify advocates who will talk for your sake. Request that your manager shares your work with his supervisor and on up the corporate hierarchy. Search for chances to expand your work to corporate pioneers. On the off chance that, similar to James, you work with customers or sellers outside your organization, request their support and referrals.

Brand yourself

You are the CEO of You, Inc. You are in charge of making your own image, for getting your name known, for being critical. You do this in many ways, large and small. Marketing "You" can be anything from building up a one of a kind signature line on your messages to turning into a specialist who is cited in industry productions and extended requests to talk at courses and gatherings.

The perception others have of you won't change overnight. What's more, once a change is made, it won't really remain as such. Making a positive impression takes your dedication, in addition to predictable activity on your part to create and refine the picture you need the world to see.

How to Covertly Plant Ideas in People's Heads Without Them Knowing It

On the off chance that you've at any point been persuaded by a salesman that you really needed an item, accomplished something too intuitively, or settled on decisions that appeared to be totally abnormal, then you've had a thought planted in your psyche. Here's the manner by which it's done.

Reverse psychology actually works

Reverse psychology has turned into a huge prosaism. I think this peaked in 1995 with the arrival of the film *Jumanji*. (In the event that you've seen it and recollect it, you hear what I'm saying.) The issue is that a great many people take a chance with reverse psychology in an exceptionally straightforward manner. For instance, you'd say "I couldn't care less; on the off chance that you need to go endanger your life bouncing out of a plane" to do whatever it takes to keep someone from going skydiving. That isn't reverse psychology—it's passive aggressive. So how about we desert all that and begin with no outside help.

If you want to utilize reverse psychology to support you, you should be inconspicuous. Suppose you need your flatmate to do the dishes, since it's his or her turn. There's this approach: "Hello, would you mind doing the dishes? It's your turn."

Be that as it may, in this case, we're accepting your flatmate is sluggish and the pleasant approach wouldn't take care of business. So, what do you do? Something like this: "Hello, I've chosen I would prefer not to do the dishes any longer and am going to begin purchasing disposable stuff. Is that cool with you? On the off chance that you can give me some cash, I can get additional items for you, as well."

What this does is divert the crappy contrasting option to not doing the dishes without casting any fault. As opposed to being engrossed with an allegation, your flatmate is left to just consider the option. This is the manner by which reverse psychology can be compelling, inasmuch as you say it like you mean it.

Never talk about the idea—talk around it

Inspiring somebody to accomplish something can be extreme, especially in the event that you know they're not going to need to do it, so you have to make them trust it was their thought. This is a typical guideline, particularly for businesspeople. However, it's significantly easier to say than do. You need to consider planting thoughts in the way you'd consider making and keeping a secret. Gradually. When an exciting secret is kept, most likely, you begin to offer the recipient a progression of intimations until the conspicuous conclusion is the one achieved. However, the key is to endure, or hold out, on the grounds that if you hurry through your "intimations" the secret will become self-evident. There is a better chance of planting thoughts, too, when you take it moderately; deftly, the thought will shape normally in their mind independent from anyone else.

Suppose you're attempting to get your companion to eat more advantageous sustenance. This is a decent point, yet you have an intense foe: they're dependent on the Colonel and need a container of broiled chicken at any rate once every day. Out of concern, you instruct them to eat more advantageous fare. They either feel that is a smart thought and after that never do anything or simply instruct you to quit pestering them. For them to acknowledge what they're doing to their body, they need an epiphany, and you can get that going by talking around the issue.

To do this, you should be exceptionally smart and extremely unobtrusive, or else it will be self-evident. You can't simply say, "Goodness, I read today that broiled chicken is killing 10 million kids in Arkansas consistently," in light of the fact that it's a heap of poop and accompanies an extraordinarily clear inspiration for saying it.

On the off chance that chicken is the objective, you have to make chicken appear to be truly unappealing. Next time you sniffle, make a joke about catching the avian influenza. When you're ordering at an eatery together, note your choice by requesting an option that is other than chicken since you recently discovered how most chicken is prepared by eateries. When you've done what's needed of these things—and, once more, with enough space between them, so it doesn't appear as odd conduct—you can begin being somewhat more forceful and quit running with your companion to get broiled chicken. You can likewise find a way to enhance your own wellbeing and tell your companion 1) what you're doing, and 2) how well it's working for you. Following half a month, if your companion hasn't chosen to reevaluate his or her position on incessant broiled chicken, you can coolly say it and they ought to be considerably more open to having a genuine dialogue.

Amplification Hypothesis

Amplification hypothesis has everything to do with the certainty of your attitude when you are talking to someone. When you display certainty, it hardens and increases someone's attitude, but when you display uncertainty, it acts by softening the attitude.

Example

A therapist wants to persuade an alcoholic to stop drinking. When the alcoholic explains why he needs his drink, the therapist vaguely agrees. When he states how negatively the drink affects, the therapist becomes more confirmatory. Here, the therapist will succeed at indirectly persuading the alcoholic by letting him see how alcoholism affects his being.

How to Use It

Align your projected attitude with that of the person you are trying to persuade. Otherwise, you will only be creating resistance.

Defending

Miss-match the persuaders attitude or be emotional when he or she is logical. That will put off the person.

Chapter 5:

The Best use of NLP or Neuro-Linguistic Programming

I n the 1970s, Richard Bandler and John Grinder developed an approach labeled NLP, or Neuro-linguistic programming. The concept was founded on the understanding that there is a link between the mind, language, and behavior of people. Changing one of these links can alter a person's ability to achieve their goals. This is because we observe our world subjectively. This means that we base "real" events according to our perception of what has happened rather than what has truly occurred. This perception is through our senses and the communication presented to us. Behavior is a response to these senses and perceptions. This means that simply changing the response to the perceptions and senses can change behavior. These responses can be both conscious and unconscious, and we need to learn how to train ourselves to respond differently to scenarios. This change of response is done through conditioning, often where a person is guided through a sequence or steps to come to a different conclusion or behavior. This concept has been applied to all sorts of behavior from smoking or addiction to common, everyday behaviors.

In order to use NLP to influence another person, there are certain steps that need to be taken:

- Establish a rapport with the other person.

- Gather information about the person's current state and where they want to go.

- Utilize tools and techniques to intervene and alter perceptions.

- Involve the proposed solutions in the client's life.

Rapport is established through verbal and nonverbal cues like mirroring a person's behavior or mannerisms. Body language is crucial at this stage. Once the rapport is developed, questions are asked to gather the information. These questions have both a verbal and nonverbal response that must be observed. Also, the other person needs to think beyond just obtaining their goal. They need to consider what will happen when they reach that goal. They need to consider both the positive and negative implications of their relationships when they reach their destination. Once the other person has decided this is still the direction they want to go, various persuasion techniques are used to change a person's conscious and unconscious responses, so they can obtain their goals. The final step is to create a way for the person to then experience what it is like when they have achieved that goal. This allows them to feel that success even before it has happened.

Neuro-Linguistic Programming (NLP)

The key NLP elements are modeling, acting, and communicating effectively. It is believed that if an individual can understand how another accomplishes a particular task, then he can copy a communicate the process to others so that they too can achieve the specific task.

The NLP proponents say that every individual has a personal reality map, and persons who practice NLP use their own and other people's perspectives to come up with a systematic overview of the situation at hand. By taking in many views, the NLP user gains more information about the situation and can make a sound judgment from it.

This belief is rooted in the premise that senses are needed for processing the information available because the mind and the body influence each other. Proponents also say that NLP is an experiential approach, which means that for a person to understand an action, he or she must perform that action to learn from the experience of performing it.

In therapy, NLP uses a set of language-based, sensory-based, and behavior-modification techniques intended to help the client improve his or her self-confidence, awareness, communication skills, and other social actions. The goal of this approach is to help the client see that the manner in which a person views the world affects how he or she operates in it.

Doing this is necessary if you are to change the behavior patterns and thoughts of the individual, to get rid of the destructive unhelpful ones.

Therapists use NLP to treat phobias and fears, stress, low self-esteem, post-traumatic stress disorder, and other mental conditions that lower the quality of life.

The idea behind this therapy is to help the client understand how his mind works. In particular, he gets to understand how he came to have the thoughts he now has, how he behaves the way he does, and how he can change his emotions and moods to reprogram his manner of processing information so that his behavior is more successful and acceptable.

Another way this therapy is helpful is that it allows the client to see how he or she has been successful in the past so that they can see just how easily they can replicate that success in the future or other spheres of their lives.

The therapist believes that the client has the answers to his problems within himself, and only conducts therapy to guide him as he draws the solutions out.

Get the Facts on Neuro-Linguistic Programming

Neuro-linguistic programming (NLP) utilizes a combination of language, neurology and programming. It is essentially a pragmatic school of thought. You will look at what successful people do and then use it to achieve something. In the case of persuasion, you will look at the behaviors of the most persuasive people and start to adopt them.

The key elements of this include action, modeling and effective communication. The premise of NLP is that if a person can understand how a person did something, they can copy their process and accomplish it too.

This technique was initially created to help people to find success in the business world. However, since its start in the 1970s, it has been adapted to work for an array of fields, including helping people to become more persuasive.

You know people who are naturally more persuasive than others. You also certainly see people in the media that can easily persuade people to do things. Of course, marketing and advertising also use NLP to promote their services and products. So, you see this technique in action daily. People take what works and use it. Simple as that.

To make NLP work for you and your persuasive abilities, you have to know what the most persuasive people are doing. Once you learn about the traits and techniques that persuasive people use, all you have to do is adopt and model them to put NLP to work.

NLP Models

There are two primary NLP models to know about. The Meta Model is a set of language patterns or specifying questions that work to expand and challenge the limits to a person's "map" of the world. This can be used to help a person decide what they ultimately want, and it teaches you which questions to ask to learn more about a situation or a person.

The Milton Model is based on language patterns and it is a type of hypnotherapy. Milton Erickson's hypnotic communication methods are used for this model. The purpose is to maintain or induce a trance, via using language, to contact the personality's hidden resources. It helps you to build a rapport with someone, cultivate unconscious communication and better use words the person you are talking to will understand and connect to.

Traits of Persuasive People

You do not have to be born naturally persuasive to be successful with it. Once you know what the best traits for this are, it will be easy to start adopting them. Once you successfully model them, you will notice it is much easier to get what you want. The traits include:

Active listening

You have surely heard about this in any communication class or seminar you have taken. When you are attempting to persuade someone to do something, they have to feel as though you have their attention. When they feel special, per se, it is much easier to get them to do something. Another element of this is once you can understand where a person is coming from, it is easier to influence them.

Effective questions

When you are talking to someone, are you asking the right questions to learn the information needed to persuade them? Make sure that your questions are open-ended and putting the other person first. This gives you a chance to learn more about their personality and how easy they will be to persuade.

You also want to make it seem like what you are asking will benefit them as much as you. Asking the right questions makes it easier to see what they view as a benefit.

Selflessness

Remember that persuasion is half you and half the person you are trying to persuade. If you put all of the focus on you, the other person no longer feels special and when this feeling disappears, so does your control over them. You want to spend the majority of the conversation on the other person. Then, you can easily add in some information about how your proposal will benefit them. By the end of the conversation, once you ask for something, they are influenced to do it.

Empathy

If someone thinks that you care, they are more likely to help you with things. This is another way to use people's emotions as a way to persuade them to do something. You learned about how powerful this technique is in a previous chapter. To be effective at using empathy, just make sure it comes across as genuine or else it can backfire on you.

Positivity

People are naturally attracted to positive people. When you give off positive energy, it is infectious, and people want more of it. They will naturally do what you want just to be in your positive presence. You see this used in sales all the time. The salespeople who are positive and upbeat are the most successful.

Confidence

It is true that people are going to respond more to a confident person. This is true even if your competence level is low. When you are confident, you can ask for things and get them without ever having to get aggressive.

Compromise

As long as you appear willing to compromise, it is easy to get what you want. You want to pick and choose when to do this. For example, stand your ground on the big things, but compromise on something small. The fact that you compromised at all will stick in the person's mind, making them easier to persuade.

Authenticity

As long as you appear authentic, people will listen to you and trust every word. When someone trusts you, they are going to want your approval and getting your approval means allowing you to persuade them to do things.

Top NLP Techniques of Persuasive People

All of the techniques that will be discussed here come from an NLP perspective and that is why they are so effective. These include:

Embedded commands

When you make it impossible to say "no" while remaining polite, you can convince people to do what you want every time. For example, do not ask a person if they want to go to dinner. Ask them where they want to go. With the first question, they can say "no," but with the second, they feel like you are wanting their opinion, so they feel compelled to have dinner with you.

Choice restriction

You want to restrict choice without it being obvious that you are doing so. For example, instead of asking a person the type of wine they would like, ask them "red or white?". The second question will restrict them to either white or red. Then, you will ultimately get to choose the wine based on the color that they chose. They will not realize that you essentially persuaded them to allow you to choose which wine the two of you are going to drink.

I could, but rather not

This is a technique you have certainly used in the past and it has likely been used on you. An example would be saying something, such as "I can drive if you want me to." At this point, you are saying you can drive, but the last part of the sentence opens the door for the other person to volunteer because you really do not want to drive. In most cases, the other person will volunteer to drive not even realizing that you wanted that exact outcome.

And vs. but

You have no idea how powerful "but" can be until you are starting to enhance your persuasion skills. This word can easily change opinions and you can fully use this to your advantage. For example, if you want someone to take you somewhere, but they are tired, you could frame it in the following way: "I know you are tired but going to this movie will be so much fun and everyone has seen it." The second part of the sentence after the "but" makes them feel obligated since the movie is trendy and fun.

What they really want

This is not only a type of NLP persuasion technique, but also a form of hypnotism. Make sure that when you ask what a person wants that you make it open. For example, ask which car they would want if money was not a factor. You can use this same approach for just about anything. Once you get their true needs and wants, you can use these to your advantage to persuade the other person to do something. For example, if you want to take a vacation with your significant other, ask where they would go if there were no restrictions. Once they answer, use this to present your idea.

Resisting Dark Persuasion with NLP

These strategies are often used, by marketing companies, governmental units, and in interpersonal relationships, to manipulate you and make you act a certain way. NLP can help you resist these attempts.

NLP is a way of working that will help you to realize your way of thinking about the world and engage with that to make changes. Remember, the map is different from the world. The world remains the same, but each person has a different map of it. NLP is all about finding how you present yourself with your map of the world.

For example, people develop different coping strategies based on what they have experienced in the past and how they got through it. There can be many ways of coping; some are what is called "adaptive" and some are what is called "maladaptive". Some are a mix of adaptive and maladaptive methods. Adaptive methods of coping are when a person finds ways to get through challenges that are healthy and propel the person closer to their authentic self. Maladaptive coping mechanisms are coping strategies, which draw people away from their authentic self and are unhealthier ways to get by. One example of an adaptive coping mechanism is creating a support structure. Let's say that a person has a good job, and then suddenly, they are laid off. This presents a challenge to the person: they must find a new job where they can get paid and do work which fits them. An example of an adaptive coping mechanism would be if this person reaches out to friends, family, and acquaintances for help. This is a strategy that the person has employed that will help them to build connections. An example of a maladaptive coping mechanism would be if this person depends on drugs to get them through this difficult time. The reason that this is maladaptive is that it will help them in the short term, by taking away the feelings of sadness or frustration that comes along with the situation. However, they start to build a dependence on drugs for treating their feelings, and eventually, they will have to find other ways to cope, as the drug use becomes unsustainable.

NLP is all about analyzing your past coping mechanisms and other patterns and being able to work in that context. You can only work in the context that works for you; if you try to use other people's strategies for dealing with challenges, you will find that you can't quite make it work.

NLP is the study of how language is connected to mental programming. Each of us tells a story when we talk. We have developed our own individualized language, which is what we created from our experiences as a person. Creating our own way of communication is one of the most unique parts of humans.

People have a language all to themselves. It is the way in which they use the English language or whichever language it is they speak. When one person says a word, they might mean something completely different than another person. This can be seen in regional differences. People in the northern United States have certain patterns of speaking and people in the southern United States have another completely different pattern of speaking. Then, beyond that, there are cultural differences. In certain cultures, people speak less directly about things. Certain phrases are learned to be sued to refer to a specific phenomenon. Learning to communicate clearly can be useful, but it is also very important to learn how to communicate within the milieu of differing cultures and different people's perspectives. You must learn how to analyze someone's speaking patterns in order to benefit from NLP.

This is a big part of NLP: creating a road map of a person's language. It is by using their own language that you can change their mind or realize when you are being persuaded. Think about a teacher who is coming into a class of kids for the first time. At first, they seem like a formal adult who is not "cool". However, if they learn to adapt to the kids' language, they are much more accepted. An adult who is very rigid in their language will not be as effective as a teacher who is able to pinpoint some of the key phrases in another person's language.

Humans tend to talk in stories. This is a key part of communication for nearly every person. People use stories to tell the world about what is happening. In fact, it is very rare that a person does not speak in stories. This is the way that we communicate and it's the way that we make understanding and meaning in the world. Telling stories is a very important part of NLP. In order to use NLP, you must be able to analyze and accept stories.

Let's think about this context for a moment. We'll use an example of an older woman, let's say about 65, who is telling you about her politics. You ask, "Why do you support Candidate X?" She tells you "Well, back in my day, people had to work hard to support themselves, and we didn't have anything handed to us. We worked hard, we lived through hard times, and we were able to get by and create something out of nothing."

Let's analyze what she said. She didn't provide you with any concrete answer, but she provided you with a lot of information. The story is what takes place of any specific points about Candidate X. This woman has a life story that she just let you a little bit in on. You can see how the story serves as the driver for the communication, rather than the specific information.

If you were to attempt to change this woman's mind, you would have to engage with her story. Her story is a common one. It is a story that older people often have. They tell that story of changing values and changing times. When they were younger, things were different, they say. They tell you about how when they were young, people had to work very hard to accomplish things that people don't have as much work to do with these days. This story may be true for them, but that doesn't mean that it is true for everyone else. That doesn't matter. In order to persuade or engage with NLP, you will have to accept the story.

This is one of the main components of NLP: acceptance. Persuasion has a lot to do with the person feeling like they are being heard, understood, and accepted. Acceptance will make a person feel safe, and when a person feels safe, they are more likely to agree with you. Accepting and validating a person's story is the first step to being able to influence them and persuade them. If you have the chance, you should dive deeper into the story.

How would you dive deeper into this woman's story? You would bring out some of the details. Where did you grow up? What did the breadwinner of your family do for work? They might have certain associations with certain types of work. Older people will sometimes no understand the complexities of modern occupations. You can think about some of the jobs that are part of the modern economy with technological companies. There are people who work for YouTube, for example, who work solely in the field of coordinating services with online companies who provide entertainment and television programs and integrate them with You tube's services. This is something that you can probably get a general idea of, but for this older woman, this doesn't make sense. She doesn't understand what YouTube really does, let alone with the integration of services like this means. This is part of the intergenerational gap that we are talking about.

In order to understand her and her story, you will have to engage with her on her level. You will have to learn how to use her language, and you can't expect her to know what you are talking about when you are talking in the vernacular of your current, modern-day situation. First, you must try to lean into the story and learn what her roadmap of the world looks like. You both live in the same world, but she will have a drastically different view of the world.

Let's use another example, this time with a very young person. Let's say they are 13 years old. Imagine the type of technology that they grew up with and they feel is natural. This will be completely different from what you grew up with. The world of technology is moving so quickly that new languages and new ways of communication are constantly evolving. This young person might have adapted to several turns of phrase and styles of communication that to you might seem very foreign.

In order to convince them, you will have to understand a little bit about their world. You would have to look into what kinds of entertainment they like if they are into sports, or music, or whatever else is relevant to that person's world. The way that a 13-year-old in this age communicates will be very different than that of a 65-year-old. They are both living in the same world, but they have completely different maps.

This subjectivity is the basis for NLP. When you realize another person's subjectivity, you are able to get inside their world. This is what the best psychotherapists do. They are able to look into a person's psyche and begin to analyze what is going on. This takes time, and many psychotherapists will require at least a few visits before they can ensure that they can work with surety and efficiency. A person will start to show their patterns after a certain amount of time. Patterns are not something that you can take hold of right away; it takes time to see how the person reacts in different circumstances and you can start to see where they have strengths and weaknesses.

Conclusion

The next step is to sit down and evaluate your persuasion skills. Once you know where you are with your skills, it will be much easier to quickly ensure that you can get your skills to the desired level. Which chapters in this book do you need to work on the most to ensure that you are as persuasive as possible? Jot down a few notes and go back to the chapters where you need improvement. Use the tips and information to make sure that you are getting more of what you want.

As you read through the chapters, you could see how powerful persuasion is. You could also see how you are persuaded to make certain choices without even realizing it. When you master the art of persuasion, you can be the person persuading others without them realizing it.

The book has also been published with the sole aim of impacting people's lives positively. Remember that you should focus on the chapters that discuss more about the strategies used by manipulative people and how you can avoid becoming a victim. After all, no one likes being manipulated by another person.

You have to keep fighting your dark side so that it does not take control over you completely. Once you know to keep off that side on edge, you will be able to identify it in others and prevent yourself from falling prey to it.

References

Bandler, Richard and Grinder, John. *Frogs into Princes*. Edited transcripts by Steve Andreas. Real People Press, 1979. Web. 2 Dec 2017.

Cialdini, Robert B. *Influence: The Psychology of Persuasion*. HarperCollins, 1993. Web. 3 Dec. 2017.

Healthline. (2020). *Psychopath: Meaning, Signs, and vs. Sociopath*. [online] Available   at: *https://www.healthline.com/health/psychopath#takeaway*.

Today, P. (2020). Changing behaviour with neuro-linguistic programming - Personnel Today. *[online] Personnel Today. Available at:* https://www.personneltoday.com/hr/changing-behaviour-with-neuro-linguistic-programming/.

Personality - Trait theories. (2020). Retrieved 2020, from *https://www.britannica.com/topic/personality/Trait-theories*

The Importance of Emotional Intelligence (Including EI Quotes). (2020). Retrieved 2020, from *https://positivepsychology.com/importance-of-emotional-intelligence/*

How to analyze people. (2020). Retrieved 2020, from *https://hubpages.com/education/How-to-analyze-people*

Explainer: how we understand people and why it's important. (2020). Retrieved 2020, from *https://theconversation.com/explainer-how-we-understand-people-and-why-its-important-26897*

Why is it important to understand personality? (2020). Retrieved 2020, from *https://preludecharacteranalysis.com/blog/why-is-it-important-to-understand-personality*

Mendoza, D., Mendoza, D., & profile, V. (2020). The Importance Of Being Able To See A Situation From Another Person's Point Of View. Retrieved 2020, from *http://danamendoza.blogspot.com/2011/11/importance-of-being-able-to-see.html*

Benefits of the Psychology of Personality. (2020). Retrieved 2020, from *https://www.ukessays.com/essays/psychology/benefits-psychology-personality-3099.php*

How to Read Body Language - Revealing Secrets Behind Nonverbal Cues. (2020). Retrieved 2020, from *https://fremont.edu/how-to-read-body-language-revealing-the-secrets-behind-common-nonverbal-cues/*

Parvez, H., & Parvez, H. (2020). Body language: Positive and negative evaluation gestures. Retrieved February 2020, from *https://www.psychmechanics.com/positive-and-negative-evaluation/*

^ *"Definition of 'Manipulate'"*. www.merriam-webster.com. Retrieved 2019-02-24.

Jump up to:*a b c d* Simon, George K (1996). In Sheep's Clothing: Understanding and Dealing with Manipulative People.*ISBN 978-1-935166-30-6*. *(reference for the entire section)*

Jump up to:*a b c* Braiker, Harriet B. (2004). Who's Pulling Your Strings ? How to Break The Cycle of Manipulation.*ISBN 978-0-07-144672-3*.

Kantor, Martin (2006). The Psychopathology of Everyday Life: How Antisocial Personality Disorder Affects All of Us.*ISBN* *978-0-275-98798-5*.

Skeem, J. L.; Polaschek, D. L. L.; Patrick, C. J.; Lilienfeld, S. O. (2011). *"Psychopathic Personality: Bridging the Gap Between Scientific Evidence and Public Policy"*.Psychological Science in the Public Interest. *12* (3): 95–162.*doi*:*10.1177/1529100611426706*. *PMID* *26167886*.

Frank, Prabbal (2007). *People Manipulation: A Positive Approach* (2 ed.). New Delhi: Sterling Publishers Pvt. Ltd (published 2009). pp. 3–7. *ISBN* *978-81-207-4352-6*. Retrieved 2019-11-09.

Clancy, Frank and Yorkshire, Heidi. "The Bandler Method." *Mother Jones* Magazine. Mother Jones, 1989. 14(2): 26. Transcription of original article in Word document. 2 Dec. 2017.

Lee, Kevan. "189 Power Words That Convert: Write Copy That Gets Your Customer's Attention Every Time." Buffer, 2 Jul. 2014. Updated 1 Dec. 2016. Web. 2 Dec. 2017.

Real, Get. "38 Convincing Words and Phrases to Adopt Immediately." 38 Convincing Words and Phrases to Adopt Immediately—推酷. N.p., n.d. Web. 12 Apr. 2017.

Stollznow, Karen. "Not-so Linguistic Programming." *Skeptic*. The Skeptics Society, 2010. 15(4): 7. Web. 2 Dec. 2017.

Zetlin, Minda. "37 Words and Phrases That Immediately Increase Your Credibility." Inc.com. Inc., 16 Nov. 2015. Web. 12 Apr. 2017.

CPSIA information can be obtained
at www.ICGtesting.com
Printed in the USA
BVHW070115280421
605952BV00014B/1951

9 781801 914888